THE ULTIMATE FOOTBALL QUIZ BOOK

Hackett Publishing

All answers correct as of Feb 2022

CONTENTS

ROUND 1 - THE PREMIER LEAGUE

ROUND 2 - THE BUNDESLIGA

ROUND 3 - THE CHAMPIONS LEAGUE

ROUND 4 - GOALKEEPERS

ROUND 5 - COPA AMERICA

ROUND 6 - GOALSCORERS

ROUND 7 - EUROPEAN CHAMPIONSHIPS

ROUND 8 - LA LIGA

ROUND 9 - THE WORLD CUP

ROUND 10 - OUTSIDE OF FOOTBALL

ROUND 11 - RIVALS

ROUND 12 - THE FIRST TO...

ROUND 13 - THE REFEREE, RED CARDS AND RULES

ROUND 14 - RECORDS

ROUND 15 - SERIE A

ROUND 16 OTHER EUROPEAN COMPETITIONS

ROUND 17 - STADIUMS

ROUND 18 - PENALTIES

ROUND 19 - TRANSFERS

ROUND 20 - AFRICA CUP OF NATIONS

ROUND 1
THE PREMIER LEAGUE

ROUND 1
THE PREMIER LEAUGE

1. In what season did the Premier League launch?

2. How many Premier League titles have Manchester United won?

3. Since the inauguration of the Premier League, the title-winning managers have come from seven different countries. Can you name them?

4. When Arsenal won the 2003/4 season without losing a game, what was the scoreline in both games against 2nd placed Chelsea?

5. Of the top 15 all-time Premier League goalscorers, 11 are English. Can you name the other four?

6. Can you name the 5 Liverpool players missing from the 2019/2020 PFA Team of the Year below?

Pope

_____   _____   Soyuncu   _____

Silva   _____   De Bruyne

Vardy   Aubameyang   _____

ROUND 1
THE PREMIER LEAUGE

7. During the 2015-16 Premier League season, Jamie Vardy set a new record for scoring in consecutive Premier League games. How many matches did he score in to break the record?

8. Can you name the eight Premier League clubs managed by Sam Allardyce?

9. How many seasons did Arsene Wenger manage Arsenal in the Premier League?

10. Can you name the two teams who have been relegated from the Premier League five times or more?

11. Who was the only player to score multiple hat-tricks during the 2019-20 Premier League season?

12. Can you name 5 players to have won the Premier League with more than one club?

13. There has only been one season of the Premier League where the three newly promoted teams were all relegated. The season was 1997-98, who were the teams?

14. Who were the 50th team to play in the Premier League?

15. Name the three players to have been sent off eight times in the Premier League?

ROUND 1
THE PREMIER LEAUGE

16. Name the Premier League stadium that has the following stands: Matthew Harding, East Stand, Shed End, West Stand

17. Which player was signed for a Premier League record £28.1 million in July 2001?

18. From 2010-11 onwards, what is Manchester City's lowest Premier League finishing position?

19. Before the start of the 2020-21 season, there were three teams who had competed in only one Premier League season. Can you name them?

20. When Sergio Aguero scored a last-minute winner to secure Manchester City's first Premier League title in 2011-12, which former Manchester City player had already been sent off in that game?

21. Who are the two teams who have played in every season of the Premier League without ever winning the title?

22. Manchester United secured the first part of their Premier League, FA Cup and Champions League treble with a 2-1 final day win over Tottenham Hotspur. Who played in goal that day?

ROUND 1
THE PREMIER LEAUGE

23. Three players with a first name beginning with 'A' have broken the Premier League transfer record. Can you name them?

24. Can you name the two players to have received over 100 yellow cards in the Premier League?

25. I experienced relegation from the Premier League with Crystal Palace, Wimbledon, Ipswich, Charlton and Portsmouth. Who am I?

ROUND 2
THE BUNDESLIGA

ROUND 2
THE BUNDESLIGA

1. With 365 goals, who is the leading goalscorer in the history of the Bundesliga?

2. Bayern Munich paid Atletico Madrid €80 million, a record fee paid for a Bundesliga club, to sign which player in 2019?

3. Which Peruvian striker holds the record for the most appearances as a non-European player in the Bundesliga?

4. At the start of the 2021-22 season, there were five founder members of the Bundesliga competing in the Bundesliga. Can you name them?

5. Which season was Hoffenheim's first in the Bundesliga?

6. Udo Lattek holds the record for the number of Bundesliga titles won as a manager. How many did he win?

7. Which player transferred for €37 million, a record transfer between clubs in the Bundesliga, in 2013?

8. Which two teams did Jurgen Klinsmann play for in the Bundesliga?

9. Who finished the 1995-96 season as the Bundesliga top scorer with 17 goals?

ROUND 2
THE BUNDESLIGA

10. In what year did the first Bundesliga match take place?

11. Which Canadian player was named in the defence in the 2020-2021 Bundesliga Team of the Season?

12. Robert Lewandowski failed to score against Greuther Furth in September 2021. How many consecutive Bundesliga games had he scored in prior to this game?

13. FC Kaiserslautern last won the Bundesliga in 1997-98. When had they last been promoted to the top flight before this championship?

14. Otto Rehhagel holds the record for the highest number of seasons managing in the Bundesliga. In total, he managed 836 games in the division, but which year was his first?

15. Who was the last Bundesliga club to win the UEFA Cup / Europa League?

16. Bayer Leverkusen have never won the Bundesliga, but how many times have they finished as runners-up?

17. Which club holds the record for the highest number of relegations from the Bundesliga?

ROUND 2
THE BUNDESLIGA

18. Which four teams qualified for the UEFA Champions League from the 2019-20 Bundesliga season?

19. Robert Lewandowski finished the 2019-20 season as the top goalscorer with 34 goals, but who was second with 28?

20. Which Hungarian goalkeeper kept the highest number of clean sheets in the Bundesliga during the 2020-21 season?

21. Bayern Munich have the largest ground capacity in the Bundesliga. What is the capacity of the Allianz Arena for domestic matches? (Nearest thousand)

22. Philip Lahm played 332 games for Bayern Munich from 2002 - 2017, but which side did he play for on loan from 2003 - 2005?

23. Which two clubs has Jurgen Klopp managed in the Bundesliga?

24. In which season was VAR first introduced in the Bundesliga?

25. How much did Borussia Dortmund pay (in euros) Polish side Lech Poznan to sign Robert Lewandowski in June 2010?

ROUND 3
THE CHAMPIONS LEAGUE

ROUND 3
THE CHAMPIONS LEAUGE

1. Can you name the three managers to have won the European Cup / Champions League three times?

2. Who was the top goal scorer in the 2000-01 Champions League?

3. In what year did the European Cup change its name to the Champions League?

4. Who were the two goalscorers in injury time when Manchester United beat Bayern Munich 2-1 at the Nou Camp in the 1998-99 Champions League final?

5. During the 2021-22 season, how many teams entered the Champions League group stage?

6. Which three languages are used in the chorus of the Champions League anthem?

7. Which city hosted the 2012-13 Champions League final between Bayern Munich and Borussia Dortmund?

8. Which two teams met in two of the first four European Cup finals?

ROUND 3
THE CHAMPIONS LEAUGE

9. Who is the only team to have never won the European Cup / Champions League but to have also lost three finals?

10. Which goalkeeper was an unused substitute in both the 2004-05 and 2020-21 Champions League Finals?

11. Which team won the European Cup in 1971, 1972 and 1973 and then won the Champions League in 1995?

12. The first European Cup took place during the 1955-56 season. Which was the first season not to have a Spanish side in the final?

13. In spite of his side being eliminated in the Round of 16, who was the top goal scorer in the 2004-05 Champions League?

14. Which team has come runners-up in the European Cup / Champions League a record 7 times?

15. Can you name the French striker who scored 28 goals in the European Cup and Champions League during spells with Marseille, Milan and Bayern Munich?

16. Who were the two goalkeepers in the 2006-07 Champions League final between AC Milan and Liverpool?

ROUND 3
THE CHAMPIONS LEAUGE

17. Which city hosted the all-English 2007-08 Champions League final between Manchester United and Chelsea?

18. Who were the three players to score 10 goals and finish as joint top goal scorers in the 2014-15 Champions League?

19. Who is the only manager to have won the Champions League with two different German sides?

20. Who were the three Brazilians to play for Inter Milan in the 2009-10 Champions League final?

21. How many European Cup finals did AC Milan reach from 1988-89 to 1994-95?

22. When was the first Champions League final to feature two teams from the same country?

23. Who are the three French clubs to have reached a European Cup / Champions League final from 1990 onwards?

24. Who refereed the 1999 Champions League final?

25. How many goals did Cristiano Ronaldo score in the 2013-14 Champions League?

ROUND 4
GOALKEEPERS

ROUND 4
GOALKEEPERS

1. Gianluigi Buffon made his first international appearance in October 1997. In what year did he make his final appearance for Italy?

2. During spells at Blackburn Rovers, Aston Villa and Tottenham Hotspur, how many consecutive Premier League games did Brad Friedel appear in?

3. Which goalkeeper was transferred from Fiorentina to Inter Milan for €28.4 million in 2001?

4. With 125 caps, Peter Shilton holds the record for the most England appearances. Which two goalkeepers have represented England in 75 games?

5. Can you name the four goalkeepers to captain their countries to World Cup glory in 1934, 1982, 2010 and 2018?

6. How old was Egypt's goalkeeper Essam El-Hadary in his last World Cup match in 2018?

7. How old was North Korea's goalkeeper Lee Chang-myung when he became the youngest goalkeeper to play in a World Cup match?

ROUND 4
GOALKEEPERS

8. Goalkeeper Jose Luis Chilavert scored 8 goals in 74 appearances for which country from 1989 - 2003?

9. The first goalkeeper to be sent off in a World Cup match was Italy's Gianluca Pagliuca against Norway in 1994. What offence did he commit to receive the red card?

10. In what year was the back-pass rule introduced?

11. Can you name the three goalkeepers who have won the Premier League 4+ times? (As of the start of the 2021/2022 season)

12. Which two goalkeepers were transferred to the Premier League for fees over £40 million in 2017 and 2018?

13. Mexican goalkeeper Antonio Carbajal played in five World Cups. Which World Cup tournament was his last?

14. Which Republic of Ireland striker went in goal and saved a penalty for Manchester City against Derby County in April 1991?

15. Peter Schmeichel played for which three Premier League teams?

ROUND 4
GOALKEEPERS

16. In what year did Manuel Neuer transfer from Schalke 04 to Bayern Munich?

17. In 1997, a law was introduced which prevented goalkeepers from holding onto the ball with their hands for longer than how many seconds?

18. In 2021, who became the first goalkeeper to score an own goal in a European Championship game?

19. I became the first goalkeeper to be transferred for £1 million when I joined Crystal Palace from Bristol Rovers in 1989. I went on to play in the Premier League for Leeds United and Everton whilst winning 23 international caps. Who am I?

20. Which German player became the first goalkeeper to win the 'Golden Ball Award' at a World Cup?

21. Fabian Barthez and Peter Shilton share the record for the highest number of clean sheets across multiple World Cups. How many clean sheets did they both keep?

22. England captain John Terry went in goal for Chelsea in a Premier League game away at Reading after which two goalkeepers had sustained head injuries?

ROUND 4
GOALKEEPERS

23. Which goalkeeper saved a shot at Wembley against England in an international friendly in 1995 with a 'scorpion kick'?

24. Patrick Battiston fell to the ground unconscious with damaged vertebrae and teeth knocked out following a challenge by which goalkeeper in the 1982 World Cup semi-final?

25. Can you name 3 of the six goalkeepers to have scored in the Premier League?

ROUND 5
COPA AMERICA

ROUND 5
COPA AMERICA

1. What was the Copa America called before 1975?

2. Which Argentinian striker finished as the tournament's leading goal scorer in 1991 and 1995?

3. Which two countries have won the competition a record 15 times?

4. Who hosted the competition and won the tournament for the first time in 2001?

5. Colombian Hernan Dario Gomez managed three countries in the Copa America from 1995 - 2019. Can you name the three countries?

6. Brazil hold the record for the most goals in a single tournament. How many goals did they score in the 1949 competition?

7. In which year was the Copa America hosted outside of South America for the first time?

8. Which country won the 1937 Copa America, beating Brazil 2-0 in the final?

ROUND 5
COPA AMERICA

9. How old was the USA's Christian Pulisic when he became the youngest player in the 2016 Copa America?

10. Who played in goal for Argentina, against Chile in the 2016 Copa America final?

11. Which country reached their only finals in 1993 and 2001 but lost both games?

12. Paraguay were beaten 3-0 by Uruguay in the 2011 Copa America final. How many games did they win in 90 mins to reach the final?

13. Which country is due to host the 2024 Copa America?

14. Which Peruvian striker finished as the leading goalscorer in the Copa America in 2011, 2015 and 2019?

15. Argentina's Guillermo Stabile coached his country in seven Copa Americas from 1941 - 1957 and holds the record for the most games as a coach. How many Copa America games did he coach in total?

16. Jamaica competed in the 2015 and 2016 Copa Americas but did not win a game in either tournament. How many goals did Jamaica score in the two competitions combined?

ROUND 5
COPA AMERICA

17. Who were the two non-Americas 'invited teams' who competed in the 2019 tournament?

18. How many Copa America tournaments did Brazilian goalkeeper Claudio Taffarel play in?

19. Brazilians won the player of the tournament award in all but one Copa America from 1997-2007. Which country did the 2001 player of the tournament, Amado Guevera, represent?

20. Which striker became the first player to score 4 goals in a Copa America game since 1959 when Chile beat Mexico 7-0 in 2016?

21. How many penalties did Argentina's Martin Palermo miss in a group stage match against Colombia in 1999?

22. In what year was Pele awarded the player of the tournament award?

23. Which Brazilian finished as the tournament's top goalscorer in 2004?

ROUND 5
COPA AMERICA

24. Brazilian and Argentinian coaches have dominated the tournament from 2004 onwards, winning all but one Copa America. The manager of the 2011 winners was of which nationality?

25. The 2015 and 2016 Copa America finals were both contested by Chile and Argentina and both went to penalties. What was the score after extra time in both games?

ROUND 6
GOALSCORERS

ROUND 6
GOALSCORERS

1. How many Premier League goals did Luis Suarez score in his 110 appearances?

2. Who won the 2014 World Cup Golden Boot?

3. Who finished Euro 2004 as the top goalscorer?

4. Which goalkeeper scored three times against Juventus and for three separate teams, in the Champions League?

5. How many goals did Oleg Salenko score for Russia in their 6-1 win over Cameroon in the group stage of the 1994 World Cup?

6. Four players shared the Golden Boot at the 2010 World Cup. Wesley Snjieder was the only one of the four to not have an 'L' in his surname. Can you name the other three?

7. In 2nd place, England's Andy Johnson was sandwiched between two Frenchmen in the Premier League's top goalscorers in 2004-05. Who were the two Frenchmen?

8. Who scored the first goal of the game in England's 5-1 victory against Germany in Munich in 2001?

9. How many goals were scored during the 2002 World Cup?

ROUND 6
GOALSCORERS

10. How much did Chelsea pay Parma to sign Gianfranco Zola in 1996?

11. Ronald Koeman and Sinisa Mihajlovic were both defenders with an eye for goal. Who scored the most international goals out of the two?

12. At the start of which season did David Beckham score against Wimbledon from the half-way line on the opening day?

13. From 2009 - 2016, I played and scored for Porto, Atletico Madrid, Monaco, Manchester United and Chelsea. Who am I?

14. Mexico hold the record for the highest number of own goals scored across all World Cups. How many have they scored?

15. How many Champions League final goals has Gareth Bale scored?

16. When Darren Bent scored for Sunderland against Liverpool in the Premier League in October 2009, what object did the ball ricochet off before ending up in the back of the net?

17. Which European country lost each game by at least three goals and failed to score in every match in the 1998 World Cup Qualifiers?

ROUND 6
GOALSCORERS

18. How much did Real Madrid pay Liverpool to sign Michael Owen in 2004?

19. How old was Lionel Messi when he made his first team debut for Barcelona in a competitive fixture?

20. In what year did AC Milan sign Andriy Shevchenko from Dynamo Kyiv?

21. Which defender equalised for Italy against France in the 2006 World Cup final?

22. Who scored in the 1992 European Championship final but only scored 1 in 99 games for Arsenal from 1992-1996?

23. In 1978, I became the first German player to score an own goal during a World Cup game. I went on to manage Germany from 1990-1998. Who am I?

24. Who were the two non-European strikers to score 20+ Premier League goals in the 2009-10 season?

25. In what year did Robbie Fowler rejoin Liverpool from Manchester City?

ROUND 7
EUROPEAN CHAMPIONSHIPS

ROUND 7
EUROPEAN CHAMPIONSHIPS

1. Who are the two countries to have won the European Championships a record three times?

2. Who were the two hosts of Euro 2000?

3. Who were the two countries to lose on penalties in the quarter-finals of Euro '96?

4. Can you complete the starting XI for France in the Euro 2000 final against Italy?

_____

_____ Blanc _____ Lizarazu

Deschamps   Viera

Djorkaeff   Zidane   _____

_____

5. Who is the only player to have scored two hat-tricks in European Championship tournaments?

ROUND 7
EUROPEAN CHAMPIONSHIPS

6. Who are the three countries to have contested only one European Championship final and to have won that final?

7. Which country hosted the 1992 Euros?

8. Which goalkeeper kept eight clean sheets in European Championship games from 2004 - 2012?

9. How many European Championships has Cristiano Ronaldo appeared in?

10. Who appeared in the final of three consecutive European Championships in 1972, 1976 and 1980?

11. How many goals did winners Greece concede during the 2004 tournament?

12. Euro 2020 took place across the continent. Which was the most eastern city to host a game?

13. Italy's Leonardo Bonucci became the oldest player to score in a Euros final when he scored against England at Wembley in 2021. How old was he at the time?

ROUND 7
EUROPEAN CHAMPIONSHIPS

14. Denmark won Euro '92 but had failed to qualify for the tournament. Whose place did they take?

15. How many times have England lost a penalty shoot-out in European Championships?

16. Who are the two individuals to have made an appearance as a player and coached in the finals of European Championships?

17. Who scored a 'golden goal' to win the final of Euro 2000?

18. Which right-sided midfielder was awarded the Man of the Match award in the Euro '96 final?

19. Three Portuguese players were suspended from UEFA competitions for a minimum of six months after ugly scenes in their defeat to France in the semi-finals of Euro 2000. Who were they?

20. True or False: Scotland played in Euro '92

21. Which 2 players started at CB for Portugal in the Euro 2016 final?

ROUND 7
EUROPEAN CHAMPIONSHIPS

22. Which European Championships tournament was the first to feature 16 teams?

23. Which Swedish referee officiated in Euro '96, Euro 2000 and Euro 2004?

24. Which England players missed penalties in the quarter-final shoot-out defeat to Portugal in 2004?

25. Who finished as top goalscorer in Euro 2016?

ROUND 8
LA LIGA

ROUND 8
LA LIGA

1. Which three teams were promoted to La Liga ahead of the 2021-22 season?

2. Three players have scored more than 200 goals in La Liga from 1990 onwards. Who are they?

3. The last season of La Liga which saw a team other than Barcelona, Real Madrid or Atletico Madrid win the title was 2002-2003. Who won La Liga that season?

4. Which Italian scored 24 league goals in 24 games for Atletico Madrid in 1997-98?

5. When did future England manager Terry Venables become Barcelona manager?

6. How many seasons did Lionel Messi finish as top scorer in La Liga?

7. Which team won the league in the 2013-14 season?

8. In what year did Pep Guardiola's Barcelona defeat Jose Mourniho's Real Madrid 5-0?

9. When did Atletico Madrid move to their new ground, the Wanda Metropolitano Stadium?

ROUND 8
LA LIGA

10. Which three teams have played in La Liga each season since it was founded in 1929?

11. How many La Liga games did Cristiano Ronaldo play for Real Madrid?

12. Two Brazilians finished as top goal scorers in La Liga across the 1992-93 and 1993-94 seasons. Who were they?

13. I joined Real Madrid from Liverpool in 1999 and played four seasons in La Liga. When I left Real Madrid in 2003, I signed for Manchester City where I played until retiring in 2005. Who am I?

14. In what season did Carlo Ancelotti win the Champions League with Real Madrid?

15. From 2009-10 to 2020-21, apart from four seasons, the winners of the UEFA Cup / Europa League were from La Liga. Which were the seasons when non-La Liga teams won the competition?

16. Where did Barcelona sign Ronaldinho from in 2003?

17. Which midfielder signed for Real Madrid from Sampdoria in 1997 before joining Middlesbrough from Real Madrid in 2000?

18. Which team has the lowest number of wins in total in La Liga since it was founded in 1929?

ROUND 8
LA LIGA

19. Real Sociedad signed their first non-Basque player in 1989. He was a striker who transferred from Liverpool. Who was it?

20. Who became the first Frenchman to finish as La Liga's top goalscorer, in 2020-21?

21. Which shirt number was Gareth Bale assigned at Real Madrid after signing for them from Tottenham Hotspur for a world record transfer fee in 2013?

22. When did Deportivo de La Coruna win their only La Liga title?

23. What is the capacity of the Camp Nou to the nearest thousand?

24. Who is the only Spanish player to finish a La Liga season as top goalscorer from 2002-03 onwards?

25. Which La Liga clubs has Rafa Benitez managed?

ROUND 9
THE WORLD CUP

ROUND 9
THE WORLD CUP

1. Which country has won the most World Cups and how many have they won?

2. There are three countries who have never won the World Cup but have lost more than one World Cup final. Can you name one of them?

3. There are four countries who have contested only one World Cup final. Can you name two of them?

4. Which country has contested the most World Cup finals?

5. Who were the two finalists in the first World Cup in 1930?

6. Who were the last team to win all of their games at a World Cup?

7. Belgium finished the 2018 World Cup as the tournament's top scorers. How many goals did they score?

8. Who were the four semi-finalists in the 1998 World Cup?

9. Who are the six countries to have won the World Cup whilst hosting the tournament?

10. In the first 1990 World Cup semi-final, what was the score between Argentina and Italy?

ROUND 9
THE WORLD CUP

11. Can you name the player who scored the opening goal of the 2010 World Cup in South Africa?

12. Which player is the overall top goal scorer across all World Cups?

13. The top goalscorers from the 1990, 1994 and 1998 World Cups all had surnames beginning with 'S'. Can you name the four players?

14. In the 1998 World Cup, Argentina's Gabriel Batistuta scored a hat-trick with goals in the 73rd, 77th and 83rd minutes. Who were Argentina playing?

15. In the 2018 World Cup, who became the first player to score a hat-trick in a drawn game?

16. Who is the only host country to have been eliminated in the first round of a World Cup?

17. Who were the four European countries to host the World Cup in 1954, 1958, 1966 and 1974?

18. Mexico have hosted the World Cup twice. In which years did they do so?

ROUND 9
THE WORLD CUP

19. Which city hosted the 2002 World Cup final?

20. Who was originally chosen to host the 1986 World Cup, but pulled out in November 1982?

21. How many times have Scotland been eliminated in the first round of a World Cup?

22. Argentina have won four of the five penalty shoot-outs they have contested in World Cups. Who beat Argentina 4-2 on penalties in the 2006 World Cup?

23. How old was Cameroon's Roger Milla when he became the oldest player to score in a World Cup in 1994?

24. Who was the first team to play in a World Cup final without scoring?

25. In the 2010 World Cup final, six players featured who played in the Premier League at that time. Can you name them?

ROUND 10
OUTSIDE OF FOOTBALL

ROUND 10
OUTSIDE OF FOOTBALL

1. Which former Manchester City striker became President of an African country in January 2018?

2. Which French World Cup winner appeared in an episode of The Bill in December 1998?

3. Which Premier League player was the 'Brylcreem Boy' from 1997 - 1999 until he shaved his hair off?

4. Who presented the UK edition of Gladiators alongside Ulrika Johnson in the 1990s?

5. Which former Crystal Palace, Manchester City and Sheffield United defender founded HQ Sports in February 2016?

6. In what sector does Robbie Fowler run an academy in which he offers a 'Beginner-Friendly Guide" to creating financial independence?

7. Which English team did former Premier League player Ramon Vega try to buy in February 2009?

8. Which sport did former Argentinian striker Gabriel Batistuta successfully take up in 2009?

ROUND 10
OUTSIDE OF FOOTBALL

9. Which former Arsenal midfielder is now a partner in GF Biochemicals and co-founded The BioJournal in October 2016?

10. Who served as Brazil's Extraordinary Minister of Sport from 1995 - 1998?

11. Former Liverpool striker Titi Camara was appointed as Sports Minister for which country in December 2010?

12. Turkey striker Hakan Sukur became an MP to the Grand National Assembly of Turkey in 2011. Which Premier League side did he play for during the 2002/2003 season?

13. Jose Mourinho was appointed as Bobby Robson's interpreter at which club in 1992?

14. Which European coach and Liverpool manager spent a year from 1969-1970 as a teaching assistant at Alsop Comprehensive School, Liverpool?

15. In what year was former England Rugby head coach Clive Woodward appointed as Performance Director at Southampton FC?

16. In 2002, which former England manager released a single for the World Cup called 'England Crazy'?

ROUND 10
OUTSIDE OF FOOTBALL

17. In what year did Ruud Gullit release his first song 'Not the Dancing Kind'? The song made it to the top 10 in Holland's charts.

18. In 2003, which two Italian players launched a fashion brand called 'Sweet Years'?

19. Former Swedish international Thomas Brolin became a 50% owner of Twinnovation AB in 1997. Which household appliance nozzles did Twinnovation specialise in?

20. True or False: Former Premier League goalkeeper Petr Cech can speak Portuguese.

21. Which sport did Ivan Perisic represent Croatia in during the summer of 2017 at the Porec Major event?

22. Which member of Manchester United's 1999 treble-winning squad released the single 'Outstanding'? The song reached number 68 in the UK singles charts in 1999.

23. Former Italian defender, Paolo Maldini, qualified for a professional tournament of which sport in 2017?

24. In 2021, which former Premier League and Real Madrid player was reported to have amassed over $100 million through poker winnings?

ROUND 10
OUTSIDE OF FOOTBALL

25. Complete the line of the first verse of the reworked version of 'Fog on The Tyne' which was released with Paul Gascoigne on vocals in October 1990?

Sitting in a sleazy snack-bar stuffing sickly _____

ROUND 11
RIVALS

ROUND 11
RIVALS

1. To the nearest million Euros, how much did Real Madrid sign Luis Figo for from rivals Barcelona in June 2000?

2. Juventus and Roma were huge rivals during the first half of the 1980s. Which side won the most Coppa Italias from 1980 - 1985?

3. Rafa Benitez became the first manager in how many years to manage both Everton and Liverpool?

4. Who were the two goalkeepers vying for the Germany No.1 jersey from 2002-2011?

5. In October 1990, two top-flight English teams were playing each other when a brawl broke out which involved 21 of the 22 players on the pitch. The teams were subsequently deducted points. Who were the teams?

6. The Milan derby is known as the 'Derby di Milano' and which other name in Italian?

7. Who scored a hat-trick as Barcelona beat Real Madrid 5-0 in January 1994?

8. How many times have England faced Germany in European Championship fixtures?

ROUND 11
RIVALS

9. Liverpool and Everton required two replays and three matches in total to determine the winner of their 1990-91 fifth round FA Cup tie. It was the last FA Cup tie to go to multiple replays before a rule change limited ties to one replay. After which of the three games did Kenny Dalglish resign as Liverpool manager?

10. Which two teams faced each other in the 1993 FA Cup final and 1993 League Cup final?

11. How many yellow cards did Tottenham Hotspur receive during the 'Battle of Stamford Bridge' in May 2016?

12. How much did Liverpool sign Nick Barmby for from Everton in 2000?

13. How many Rome derbies did Francesco Totti play in?

14. Which Brazilian scored in four successive El Classico La Liga matches from 2004 - 2006?

15. Which teams contest 'Der Klassiker' in German football?

16. Liverpool and Chelsea clashed over two legs in the 2005 Champions League semi-final. Who scored the only goal of the two legs with a strike which has long been argued to have not crossed the line?

ROUND 11
RIVALS

17. Uruguayan Enrique Fernandez became the first coach to manage both Real Madrid and Barcelona. Which Serbian managed Real Madrid in the early 1990s and Barcelona in 2003?

18. The 'Superclasico' in Argentina refers to a game between which two sides?

19. Manchester United had four first-team strikers during their treble-winning season of 1998-1999. Which two had fallen out and did not speak to each other off the field?

20. Where did Roy Keane and Patrick Vieira have to be separated before the Arsenal v Manchester United clash in February 2005?

21. In what year did Pep Guardiola and Jurgen Klopp first manage sides against each other?

22. Which ground hosted the all-North London FA Cup semi-final in 1991?

23. How much did Sol Campbell cost Arsenal when he moved from North London rivals Tottenham Hotspur in 2001?

24. Everton beat Liverpool at Anfield in February 2021 for the first time since 1999. Who scored for Everton in their 1-0 win in September 1999?

ROUND 11
RIVALS

25. The most played World Cup fixture is shared between Germany v Argentina and Brazil v Sweden. How many times have both fixtures been played in World Cups?

ROUND 12
THE FIRST TO...

ROUND 12
THE FIRST TO...

1. Milorad Arsenijevic was the first to both play and manage in World Cups. Which country did he play for and manage in World Cup tournaments?

2. Lee Martin scored the only goal in the FA Cup final Replay to secure Alex Ferguson's first major trophy as Manchester United manager. What season was this?

3. Who was the first 'big money' player to sign for Manchester City after they were taken over by Sheikh Mansour?

4. Who was the first player to score in the 2006 World Cup?

5. Charlie Wallace was the first player to miss a penalty in an FA Cup final in 1913. Which team was he playing for?

6. Who was the first manager to win the FA Cup at the new Wembley Stadium in 2007?

7. Who were the first and only Greek side to reach the European Cup / Champions League final?

8. What was the score in the first game of the 2020 European Championships between Turkey and Italy?

ROUND 12
THE FIRST TO...

9. Uruguayan right-back Maxi Pereira was the first player to be sent off in the 2014 World Cup. Who were Uruguay playing in that game?

10. In what year did the first post-WWII World Cup take place?

11. Who were the first English League Cup winners of the new century in 2000?

12. Which World Cup was the first to see teams from Asia, Europe, North America, Africa and South America reach the second round?

13. Who became the first European country to win a World Cup played outside of Europe?

14. Which World Cup saw the first game played indoors?

15. When Arsenal reached the Champions League final in 2006, who were the two English players in their squad?

16. In which year did Cristiano Ronaldo score his first goal for Portugal?

17. Ian Porterfield was the first Premier League manager to be sacked. Which team was he sacked from?

ROUND 12
THE FIRST TO...

18. The first European Cup Final to finish 0-0 was in 1985-86. Who were the two teams in the final?

19. Robert Prosinecki became the first player to score for two different countries in World Cups. Who were the two countries?

20. Louis Saha played for six teams in the Premier League. In 1999, which English club did he sign for on loan?

21. In which World Cup tournament was the FIFA World Cup Trophy awarded to the winners instead of the Jules Rimet Trophy?

22. Who did Michael Owen score his first international goal against in a friendly before the 1998 World Cup?

23. Cristiano Ronaldo was the only player to score 30 Premier League goals in 2007-08. Who were the other two players to score 20+ Premier League goals that season?

24. Which was the first World Cup to occur without any player scoring a hat-trick?

25. In which year did Diego Maradona score his first goal for Argentina in a 3-1 victory over Scotland at Hampden Park?

ROUND 13
THE REFEREE, RED CARDS AND RULES

ROUND 13
THE REFEREE, RED CARDS AND RULES

1. Up until 2000, a goalkeeper was restricted to how many steps when handling the ball?

2. Which referee appeared on the front cover of the Pro Evolution 3 and Pro Evolution 4 video games?

3. How many yellow cards did English referee Graham Poll issue to Croatia's Josip Simunic before sending him off in the 2006 World Cup?

4. What nationality was the referee in the 1966 World Cup final?

5. In what year did Said Belqola become the first African to referee a World Cup final?

6. Excluding travelling expenses, how much were the referee and assistant referees paid for officiating in the 2013-14 FA Cup final?

7. How many red cards were issued during the 2006 World Cup second round game between The Netherlands and Portugal?

8. Which Argentinian player in 2002 became the first player to be sent off in a World Cup game after coming on as a substitute?

9. Red and yellow cards were first introduced in which World Cup?

ROUND 13
THE REFEREE, RED CARDS AND RULES

10. Who pushed referee Paul Alcock after receiving a red card in the Premier League in September 1998?

11. What were the two offences for which Zinedine Zidane was dismissed in the 1998 and 2006 World Cups?

12. How many metres from the goal line is the penalty spot in 11-aside football?

13. What was the nationality of the referee who dismissed David Beckham against Argentina in the 1998 World Cup?

14. I refereed the Champions League final between Atletico Madrid and Real Madrid and became Saudi Arabia's Head of Refereeing in 2017. Who am I?

15. In what year did Howard Webb referee the World Cup Final?

16. Who became the first player to be sent off in a Champions League final in 2006?

17. How many times was Roy Keane sent off in his playing career?

18. Between 1990 and 2010, which were the only two World Cup final games to not have a player sent off?

ROUND 13
THE REFEREE, RED CARDS AND RULES

19. A Swedish referee was struck by a coin from the stands and abandoned a Champions League game in 2004. Where was the game taking place?

20. What alteration was made to the offside rule by the International Football Association Board in June 1907?

21. Who became the first Premier League manager (not including player-managers) to be shown a yellow card in the 2019 Community Shield?

22. Which three South American countries have had the most players sent off in World Cup tournaments?

23. Which Cameroon player was sent off in successive World Cup tournaments in 1994 and 1998?

24. To the nearest metre, what are the dimensions of an adult 11-aside goal?

25. In which year was VAR first used in the FA Cup final?

ROUND 14
RECORDS

ROUND 14
RECORDS

1. Robert Lewandowski finished as the Bundesliga top goalscorer in all but one year from 2014 - 2020. Which year did he miss out?

2. How many goals did Mexican goalkeeper Jorge Campos score from non-set pieces?

3. Iker Casillas made 192 international club competition appearances until 2019. In which year did he make his first?

4. Nathan Pond was recognised in the Guinness World Record Book as appearing in the most different divisions with a single football club. How many divisions did he play in for Fleetwood Town?

5. Pep Guardiola completed a double treble when he won six trophies as the manager of Barcelona in 2009. Which trophies did he win?

6. Who are the only two teams to have gone through an entire English top-flight league season without losing a game?

7. Who played in three consecutive World Cup finals from 1994 - 2002?

ROUND 14
RECORDS

8. Excluding covid-19 restrictions, the lowest attendance in a Premier League game was recorded in January 1993. Who were the two teams playing?

9. In 2011, the record for the longest headed goal was broken. At how many metres does the record stand?

10. Which German player won the FIFA World Player of the Year award in 1991?

11. Who was the only player apart from Cristiano Ronaldo and Lionel Messi to win the Ballon d'Or from 2008 - 2021?

12. How many places below Tottenham Hotspur were Marine when they played them in the 2021 FA Cup third round?

13. Which country has the highest winning game % in the European Championships?

14. Who is the only non-British player to have appeared in 500+ Premier League games?

15. England scored at least one goal in how many consecutive European Championship games from 1996 - 2012?

ROUND 14
RECORDS

16. Which teams played in front of a record 83,222 spectators in the Premier League in February 2018?

17. How many FA Cup finals have Newcastle United reached?

18. Who were the first team to reach 100 red cards in the Premier League?

19. Who was the last Ajax player to finish in the Ballon d'Or top 3?

20. Which player scored against 17 of the 20 Premier League teams in 1996-97?

21. Which non-league side became the first to reach the FA Cup sixth round in 2016-17?

22. Who is the only English player Chelsea have sold for over £30m

23. True or false, over 70 countries have played in World Cups?

24. How many goals in total did Lionel Messi score for club and country in 2012?

25. Two teams have had the Premier League Golden Boot winner from their team on at least six occasions. Who are the two teams?

ROUND 15
SERIE A

ROUND 15
SERIE A

1. Four players have appeared in over 600 Serie A games. Can you name them?

2. No team apart from Juventus, Inter Milan or AC Milan have won Serie A since the 2000-01 season. Who won the league in 2001?

3. Which French player finished as the top goalscorer in Serie A for three successive seasons from 1983 - 1985?

4. How many teams played in Serie A each season from 1988 - 2004?

5. Which is the only season that Juventus spent outside of Serie A?

6. The 2002-03 Champions League final featured two Italian teams. Who were they?

7. From 2005 - 2012, the top goalscorer in Serie A was Italian in all but two seasons. Who was the non-Italian player to finish as top goalscorer in 2008-09 and 2011-12?

8. I played 396 times and scored 58 goals in Serie A for Sampdoria, Inter Milan and AC Milan. I also played 121 times for Real Madrid and was born in Suriname. My final appearance in Serie A was in 2012. Who am I?

ROUND 15
SERIE A

9. The last time a Serie A club held the world record transfer fee paid was in 2000 when Lazio signed which player from Parma?

10. Which two Serie A clubs did Gianluca Vialli play for?

11. Venezia were promoted to Serie A as Serie B play-off winners from the 2020-21 season. They have the smallest stadium capacity in Serie A. To the nearest thousand, how many people can the Stadio Pier Luigi Penzo hold?

12. Andrea Pirlo is the only player to have won the Serie A Footballer of The Year award in three successive seasons. Which seasons did he win it?

13. No player had done it since 1959, but what did Luca Toni do for Fiorentina in 2005-06 and Gonzalo Higuain for Napoli in 2015-16?

14. Paul Gascoigne played in Serie A for Lazio from 1992 - 1995. Which team sold him to Lazio and which team did Lazio sell him to?

15. Swedish coach Niels Liedholm won Serie A in 1979 and 1983. Who became the second Swedish manager to win Serie A in 2000?

ROUND 15
SERIE A

16. How old was goalkeeper Gianluigi Donnarumma when he made his Serie A debut in October 2015?

17. How many consecutive seasons did Andriy Shevchenko play for AC Milan?

18. I managed AC Milan twice, Real Madrid twice as well as Roma and Juventus in Serie A. I also managed England and Russia. Who am I?

19. Inter Milan signed Ronaldo from Barcelona for a world-record transfer fee in 1997. How much did they buy him for?

20. Pierluigi Casiraghi signed for Chelsea from which Serie A club in May 1998?

21. Can you complete Juventus' starting XI from the 2016/2017 Champions League final?

Buffon

Chiellini _____ Barzagli

Alves   Khedira   Pjanic   Sandro

Dybala

_____   _____

ROUND 15
SERIE A

22. How many Serie A titles did Giovanni Trappattoni win?

23. Who is the only Brazilian player to win the Serie A Footballer of the Year Award this century?

24. Which teams finished in the top four of Serie A in 2020-21?

25. Who managed Inter Milan from 2008 - 2010?

ROUND 16
OTHER EUROPEAN COMPETITIONS

ROUND 16
OTHER EUROPEAN COMPETITIONS

1. Which five English clubs lost in the final of the UEFA Cup or Europa League from 2000 onwards?

2. Who won the Cup Winners Cup final in 1999?

3. Which was the first season of the Europa League?

4. The UEFA Super Cup was launched in 1973 as a one-off game between the winners of the European Cup and the winners of the UEFA Cup. However, it wasn't until 1990 that two clubs from the same country contested the trophy. They were both Italian sides. Who were they?

5. Which country has provided the most UEFA Cup / Europa League winners?

6. In what year was the UEFA Cup launched?

7. English teams won the Cup Winners Cup more than any other. How many did they win?

8. Who were the only two English players in the Manchester United starting XI in their Europa League final win over Ajax in May 2017?

9. Which country did the 2008 Super Cup winners come from?

ROUND 16
OTHER EUROPEAN COMPETITIONS

10. Which team has won the Europa League / UEFA Cup 6 times since 2006?

11. Who did Liverpool beat in the 2000/2001 UEFA Cup final?

12. Real Madrid never won the Cup Winners Cup but how many finals did they play in?

13. Which French club share the record of three Europa League / UEFA Cup final defeats from 1999 onwards?

14. From 2013 - 2021, how many of the 9 UEFA Super Cup matches went to extra-time?

15. How much prize money will/did the 2021-22 Europa League Champions receive for winning the final?

16. Can you name the three Scottish clubs to have lost their only UEFA Cup final appearances?

17. Who scored the winning goal for Barcelona in their 1-0 win over Paris Saint Germain in the 1997 Cup Winners Cup final?

18. Which city hosted the 2011 all-Portuguese Europa League final?

ROUND 16
OTHER EUROPEAN COMPETITIONS

19. Who scored the only goal of the 1999 Super Cup between Chelsea and Real Madrid?

20. Unai Emery has won the Europa League four times as a manager since 2014. Which two sides has he won the tournament with?

21. Which was the last season that saw the UEFA Cup final played over two legs?

22. Three English clubs won the Cup Winners Cup during the 1990s. Can you name them?

23. When was the last time that an English manager won the UEFA Cup / Europa League?

24. The UEFA Super Cup was hosted by who from 1998 - 2012?

25. What was the final score on penalties in the 2020-21 Europa League final?

ROUND 17
STADIUMS

ROUND 17
STADIUMS

1. Which 2021/2022 Premier League stadium has the lowest capacity?

2. Since 2001, what is the FIFA minimum stadium capacity for World Cup games?

3. What are the three largest stadiums, by capacity, in Europe?

4. All FA Cup semi-finals have been played at Wembley since 2008. Which three venues were most used as neutral stadiums for FA Cup semi-finals before 2008?

5. In October 2017, what did the Amsterdam Arena change its name to?

6. Which Bundesliga club's stadium sold out 99.7% of their seats during the 2019-20 season?

7. In November 2020, what was forbidden at the San Siro by a new rule from the local government?

8. In what year did the Bradford City stadium fire occur?

9. How many venues were there during the 2002 World Cup?

ROUND 17
STADIUMS

10. Mountain rescue techniques had to be used, due to the steepness of one of the stands, during test events at which Euro 2000 stadium?

11. At the end of which season did Arsenal leave Highbury?

12. Which two stadiums have hosted two World Cup finals?

13. Which club has played in the most home stadiums during the Premier League era?

14. At 0.2 miles apart, which clubs have the two closest professional football grounds in the UK?

15. The record attendance in a European Championship fixture is 79,115 at the Bernabeu Stadium in 1964. Which two countries were playing?

16. True or False: The Rookery Stand is a stand at the home of Everton, Goodison Park.

17. Which city hosted the most northern venue used in the 1966 World Cup?

18. Juventus and Torino left the Stadio delle Alpi in 2006. Which year did they move in?

ROUND 17
STADIUMS

19. Which city hosted the most northern stadium used during the 2006 World Cup?

20. How many of the 18 Bundesliga clubs either lowered or froze their ticket prices in 2016-17?

21. Which stadium hosted the FA Cup final from 2001 - 2006?

22. Which ground had the lowest capacity in the first season of the Premier League?

23. Which city hosted the 2008 European Championship final?

24. David Beckham and Paul Scholes made their Manchester United debuts in September 1994 at a ground 29 miles from Old Trafford. Which ground was it?

25. Which GB Olympic Champion had a stand named after her at Bramall Lane from 2012 - 2015?

ROUND 18
PENALTIES

ROUND 18
PENALTIES

1. What year was the idea of a penalty kick approved by the International Football Association Board?

2. Who holds the record for the most number of penalties scored in the Premier League?

3. Who, after scoring for Croatia earlier in the game, gave away the first-ever World Cup final VAR penalty by being adjudged to have handled the ball in his penalty area against France in 2018?

4. How many consecutive penalties were scored in the penalty shoot-out to decide the 2021 Europa League final between Villarreal and Manchester United?

5. Which World Cup saw the first penalty shoot-out?

6. What is the ABBA sequence in a penalty shoot-out?

7. Who was the first goalkeeper to save a penalty in an FA Cup final?

8. Which outfield player has participated in a record three penalty shoot-outs in World Cup fixtures?

9. Which England player faced the opposite goal throughout the Euro 96 semi-final penalty shoot-out against Germany?

ROUND 18
PENALTIES

10. How does a referee indicate the awarding of a penalty kick?

11. Who holds the record for the highest number of penalties scored in Serie A?

12. Who scored the winning penalty in the 2005 FA Cup final?

13. In what year did Antonin Panenka score his famous penalty against West Germany to win the European Championship?

14. What did Portugal goalkeeper Ricardo remove before saving the final England penalty in the 2004 European Championship?

15. During which World Cup were penalty shoot-outs required in both semi-finals?

16. Who was the only player to miss a penalty during the 1992 European Championship semi-final shoot-out between Denmark and the Netherlands?

17. Which country has been awarded the most penalties in World Cup games?

18. Which country holds the record for the most World Cup knockout games played without contesting a penalty shoot-out?

ROUND 18
PENALTIES

19. The 2018 World Cup saw the most penalties awarded, scored and missed. How many were awarded in total?

20. Which two England players missed penalties during the 1998 World Cup second round penalty shoot-out against Argentina?

21. Which goalkeeper used 'spaghetti legs' to distract the opposition in the 1984 European Cup final penalty shoot-out?

22. Can you name the two players to have scored penalties in the Premier League with both feet?

23. Which two countries, who had both previously won all three of their World Cup penalty shoot-outs, required a penalty shoot-out to decide who progressed to the 2006 semi-final?

24. What offence did Luis Suarez commit to give away a penalty in the final minute of extra time against Ghana in the 2010 World Cup quarter-final?

25. Which two Italian players missed penalties during the 2020 European Championship final penalty shoot-out against England?

ROUND 19
TRANSFERS

ROUND 19
TRANSFERS

1. In what year was the Bosman rule introduced?

2. At the end of the 1980s, who was the most expensive footballer on the planet?

3. Real Madrid paid a world record transfer fee on five occasions from 2000 - 2013. Who were the five record-breaking signings?

4. Which Belgian international has commanded cumulative transfer fees of £293.5 million over five transfers from 2011 - 2021.

5. I played for Leeds United and Newcastle United before transferring to Real Madrid in 2004. I then returned to England with Middlesbrough before going on to play for Tottenham Hotspur, Stoke City and finally for Middlesbrough again. Who am I?

6. At the start of the 2021-22 season, who was the most expensive German footballer?

7. Which Argentinian striker transferred between two Italian clubs for a fee of €90 million in 2016?

8. How much did Manchester United sign Harry Maguire for from Leicester City in 2019?

ROUND 19
TRANSFERS

9. Christian Vieri was the most expensive player at the turn of the century. Who did he sign for Inter Milan from?

10. Who did Manchester United sign for £505,000 from FC Brondby in 1991?

11. From 1952 - 1996, Italian clubs and one other side on three occasions, held the world record for transfer fee paid. Who was the other non-Italian side who broke the record in 1973, 1982 and 1996?

12. Chinese Super League side Shanghai SIPG broke the transfer record fee paid for a non-European side when they signed which player from Chelsea in 2017?

13. Can you name the three players to transfer from Manchester United to Arsenal during the Premier League era?

14. After playing for Manchester United from 2007 - 2009, which player then represented Manchester City from 2009 - 2013?

15. Who were the selling and buying clubs when Denilson broke the world record transfer fee in 1998?

16. Which Premier League club was banned from signing players for two transfer windows in November 2019?

ROUND 19
TRANSFERS

17. True or False: Nicolas Anelka transferred from AC Milan to Juventus.

18. Which German central midfielder signed for Real Madrid from VfB Stuttgart in 2010?

19. Signed by Newcastle United in 2019, who is the most expensive outbound transfer from Major League Soccer?

20. After which international tournament did Karel Poborsky sign for Manchester United and Patrik Berger sign for Liverpool?

21. Which three Italian clubs purchased England captain David Platt during the 1990s?

22. Which Danish player transferred from Barcelona to Real Madrid in 1994?

23. Paul Pogba signed for Manchester United from Juventus for a fee of £89.3 million in 2016. But how much had Juventus paid Manchester United for Pogba four years earlier?

24. Roman Abramovich bought Chelsea in the summer of 2003. Who was their first signing for £6 million from West Ham United?

25. In what year did Neymar move from Barcelona to Paris Saint Germain for a fee of around £200 million?

ROUND 20
AFRICA CUP OF NATIONS

ROUND 20
AFRICA CUP OF NATIONS

1. Which country has won the Africa Cup of Nations a record seven times?

2. The first Africa Cup of Nations was hosted by Sudan. In what year did it take place?

3. Cameroon beat Senegal on penalties in the 2002 Africa Cup of Nations final. Which countries did the two managers come from?

4. What was the final score on penalties when Ivory Coast beat Ghana on penalties in the 2015 Africa Cup of Nations final?

5. What age was Hossam Hassan when he scored for Egypt against DR Congo in February 2006 to become the oldest goalscorer in an Africa Cup of Nations?

6. At the end of the 2019 Africa Cup of Nations, who was the all-time top goalscorer across all tournaments?

7. How many teams competed in the 1994 Africa Cup of Nations?

8. Which country will host the Africa Cup of Nations for the first time in 2025?

9. In which decade did Ghana win the Africa Cup of Nations in successive tournaments?

ROUND 20
AFRICA CUP OF NATIONS

10. In which year did Kolo Toure make his first Africa Cup of Nations appearance?

11. I won the Champions League in 1994-95 and played in six Africa Cup of Nations from 2000 - 2010. I got an Olympic Gold Medal in 1994 and won the FA Cup final in 2008. Who am I?

12. In which year did Ghana and Nigeria become the first co-hosts of the Africa Cup of Nations?

13. Can you name the English manager who won the 1986 Africa Cup of Nations?

14. I was born in Lyon and played 6 games for France U-21 before scoring 7 goals for Mali in the Africa Cup of Nations from 2004 - 2010. I played for West Ham United and Tottenham Hotspur in the Premier League from 2000 - 2005. Who am I?

15. The second Africa Cup of Nations saw a European coach win the tournament. What nationality was the coach?

16. Which country hosted and won their debut Africa Cup of Nations in 1996?

17. How many goals did Didier Drogba score in the Africa Cup of Nations?

ROUND 20
AFRICA CUP OF NATIONS

18. Asamoah Gyan made his Africa Cup of Nations debut in which tournament?

19. Who appeared in eight Africa Cup of Nations for Cameroon from 1996 - 2010?

20. Which non-African country has provided the winning manager of the Africa Cup of Nations on five occasions?

21. I finished as the joint top goalscorer in the 1998 Africa Cup of Nations with 7 goals and was also given the Most Valuable Player Award. From 2006 - 2010, I scored 37 goals in 109 games for Blackburn Rovers. Who am I?

22. What age was Egypt's Essam El Hadary when he played against Cameroon in the 2017 Africa Cup of Nations final? He is the oldest player to appear in an Africa Cup of Nations fixture.

23. Who was the first team to play 100 games at the Africa Cup of Nations?

24. When was the last Africa Cup of Nations tournament to not feature Tunisia?

25. Which two countries co-hosted the 2012 Africa Cup of Nations?

ANSWER PAGES

ROUND 1 - THE PREMIER LEAGUE
1. 1992/3
2. 13
3. Scotland, Italy, Spain, France, Portugal, Chile, Germany
4. 2-1 to Arsenal
5. Sergio Aguero (Argentina), Thierry Henry (France), Robin van Persie (Netherlands), Jimmy Floyd Hasselbaink (Netherlands)
6. Alexander-Arnold, Van Dijk, Robertson, Henderson, Mane
7. 11
8. Bolton Wanderers, Newcastle United, Blackburn Rovers, West Ham United, Sunderland, Everton, Crystal Palace, West Bromwich Albion
9. 22 (1996/97 - 2017/18)
10. Norwich City and West Bromwich Albion
11. Raheem Sterling
12. Any of: Henning Berg, Nicolas Anelka, Ashley Cole, Riyadh Mahrez, Robert Huth, Mark Schwarzer, Gael Clichy, James Milner, Carlos Tevez, Kolo Toure, N'Golo Kante
13. Bolton Wanderers, Barnsley, Crystal Palace
14. Brentford
15. Duncan Ferguson, Richard Dunne, Patrick Vieira
16. Stamford Bridge
17. Juan Sebastian Veron
18. Fourth 2015/16
19. Barnsley, Blackpool, Swindon Town
20. Joey Barton
21. Everton, Tottenham Hotspur
22. Peter Schmeichel
23. Andy Cole, Alan Shearer, Andriy Shevchenko
24. Gareth Barry, Wayne Rooney
25. Herman Hreidarsson

ROUND 2 - THE BUNDESLIGA
1. Gerd Muller
2. Lucas Hernandez
3. Claudio Pizarro
4. Borussia Dortmund, Eintracht Frankfurt, Hertha BSC, FC Koln, VfB Stuttgart
5. 2008-2009
6. 8
7. Mario Gotze
8. VfB Stuttgart, Bayern Munich
9. Fredi Bobic
10. 1963
11. Alphonso Davies
12. 15
13. 1996-97
14. 1974
15. Schalke 04 (1996-97)
16. 5
17. FC Nürnberg
18. Bayern Munich, Borussia Dortmund, RB Leipzig, Borussia Mönchengladbach
19. Timo Werner
20. Peter Gulacsi
21. 75,000
22. VfB Stuttgart
23. Mainz 05, Borussia Dortmund
24. 2017-18
25. €4.5 million

ROUND 3 - THE CHAMPIONS LEAGUE

1. Paisley, Ancelotti, Zidane
2. Raul
3. 1992
4. Sheringham, Solskjaer
5. 32
6. German, French, English
7. London
8. Real Madrid, Stade Reims
9. Atletico Madrid
10. Scott Carson
11. Ajax
12. 1962-63
13. Ruud van Nistelrooy
14. Juventus
15. Jean Pierre Papin
16. Dida, Pepe Reina
17. Moscow
18. Ronaldo, Neymar, Messi
19. Ottmar Hitzfeld
20. Julio Cesar, Maicon, Lucio
21. 5
22. 1999-2000 (Real Madrid vs Valencia)
23. Marseille, Monaco, PSG
24. Pierluigi Collina
25. 17

ROUND 4 - GOALKEEPERS

1. 2018
2. 310
3. Francesco Toldo
4. David Seaman, Joe Hart
5. Gianpiero Combi, Dino Zoff, Iker Casillas, Hugo Lloris
6. 45 years, 161 days
7. 19 years, 191 days
8. Paraguay
9. Handling the ball outside the penalty area
10. 1992
11. Peter Schmeichel, Petr Cech, Edwin van der Sar
12. Allison, Kepa
13. 1966
14. Niall Quinn
15. Manchester United, Aston Villa, Manchester City
16. 2012
17. 6
18. Wojciech Szczęsny
19. Nigel Martyn
20. Oliver Kahn
21. 10
22. Petr Cech, Carlo Cudicini
23. Rene Higuita
24. Harald Schumacher
25. Alisson, Begovic, Schmeichel, Robinson, Howard, Friedel

ROUND 5 - COPA AMERICA

1. South American Football Championship
2. Gabriel Batistuta
3. Uruguay, Argentina
4. Colombia
5. Colombia, Ecuador, Panama
6. 46
7. 2016
8. Argentina
9. 17 Years Old
10. Sergio Romero
11. Mexico
12. Zero
13. Ecuador
14. Paolo Guerrero
15. 44
16. Zero
17. Japan, Qatar
18. 5
19. Honduras
20. Eduardo Vargas
21. 3
22. 1959
23. Adriano
24. Uruguayan
25. 0-0

ROUND 6 - GOALSCORERS

1. 69
2. James Rodriguez
3. Milan Baros
4. Hans-Jorg Butt
5. Five
6. Thomas Muller, David Villa, Diego Forlan
7. Thierry Henry, Robert Pires
8. Carsten Jancker
9. 161
10. £4.5 million
11. Koeman (14)
12. 1996-97
13. Radamel Falcao
14. Four
15. Three
16. A Beach Ball
17. San Marino
18. £8 million
19. 17
20. 1999
21. Marco Matterazzi
22. John Jensen
23. Berti Vogts
24. Didier Drogba, Carlos Tevez
25. 2006

ROUND 7 - EUROPEAN CHAMPIONSHIPS

1. Germany, Spain
2. Belgium, Netherlands
3. Spain, Netherlands
4. GK Barthez, RB Thuram, CB Desailly, LF Henry, CF Dugarry
5. Michael Platini
6. Netherlands (1988), Denmark (1992), Greece (2000)
7. Sweden
8. Iker Casillas
9. 5
10. Rainer Bonhof
11. 4
12. Baku
13. 34 years, 71 days
14. Yugoslavia
15. 5
16. Dino Zoff, Didier Deschamps
17. David Trezeguet
18. Karel Poborsky
19. Abel Xavier, Nuno Gomes, Paulo Bento
20. True
21. Jose Fonte, Pepe
22. Euro '96
23. Anders Frisk
24. Beckham, Vassell
25. Antoine Griezmann (6)

ROUND 8 - LA LIGA

1. Espanyol, Mallorca, Rayo Vallecano
2. Cristiano Ronaldo, Lionel Messi, Raul
3. Valencia
4. Christian Vieri
5. 1984
6. 8
7. Atletico Madrid
8. 2010
9. 2017
10. Real Madrid, Barcelona, Athletic Bilbao
11. 292
12. Bebeto, Romario
13. Steve McManaman
14. 2013-14
15. 2010-11, 2012-13, 2016-17, 2018-19
16. Paris Saint Germain
17. Christian Karembeu
18. Cultural Leonesa (5 wins)
19. John Aldridge
20. Karim Benzema
21. 11
22. 1999-2000
23. 99,000
24. Daniel Guiza
25. Real Valladolid, Extremadura, Valencia, Real Madrid

ROUND 9 - THE WORLD CUP

1. Brazil, 5
2. Hungary (2), Czechoslovakia (2), Netherlands (3)
3. Spain, England, Sweden, Croatia
4. Germany (8)
5. Argentina and Uruguay
6. Brazil 2002
7. 16
8. Brazil, France, Croatia, The Netherlands
9. Uruguay (1930), Italy (1934), England (1966), West Germany (1974), Argentina (1978), France (1998)
10. 1-1
11. Siphiwe Tshabalala
12. Miroslav Klose (16)
13. Salvatore Schillaci, Oleg Salenko, Hristo Stoichkov, Davor Suker
14. Jamaica
15. Cristiano Ronaldo (Spain 3-3 Portugal)
16. South Africa (2010)
17. Switzerland, Sweden, England, West Germany
18. 1970, 1986
19. Yokohoma
20. Colombia
21. 8 (1954, 1958, 1974, 1978, 1982, 1986, 1990, 1998)
22. Germany
23. 42
24. Argentina, 1990
25. Heitinga, De Jong, Kuyt, Van Persie, Fabregas, Torres

ROUND 10 - OUTSIDE OF FOOTBALL

1. George Weah
2. Emmanuel Petit
3. David Beckham
4. John Fashanu
5. Sun Jihai
6. Property
7. Portsmouth
8. Polo
9. Mathieu Flamini
10. Pele
11. Guinea
12. Blackburn Rovers
13. Sporting Lisbon
14. Gerard Houllier
15. 2005
16. Terry Venables
17. 1984
18. Paolo Maldini, Christian Vieri
19. Vacuum Cleaner
20. False
21. Beach volleyball
22. Andy Cole
23. Tennis (Doubles)
24. Thomas Gravesen
25. Sausage Rolls

ROUND 11 - RIVALS

1. €62 million
2. Roma
3. 129 years
4. Jens Lehmann, Oliver Kahn
5. Manchester United, Arsenal
6. Derby della Madonnina
7. Romario
8. Three
9. Second
10. Arsenal, Sheffield Wednesday
11. Nine
12. £6 million
13. 44
14. Ronaldinho
15. Bayern Munich, Borussia Dortmund
16. Luis Garcia
17. Radomir Antic
18. River Plate, Boca Juniors
19. Andy Cole, Teddy Sheringham
20. The tunnel
21. 2013
22. Wembley
23. He Was A Free Transfer
24. Kevin Campbell
25. Seven

ROUND 12 - THE FIRST TO...

1. Yugoslavia
2. 1989-90
3. Robinho
4. Philip Lahm
5. Aston Villa
6. Jose Mourinho
7. Panathinaikos
8. Turkey 0 - 3 Italy
9. Costa Rica
10. 1950
11. Leicester City
12. 2002
13. Spain (2010)
14. 1994
15. Sol Campbell, Ashley Cole
16. 2004
17. Chelsea
18. Steaua Bucharest, Barcelona
19. Yugoslavia, Croatia
20. Newcastle United
21. 1974
22. Morocco
23. Torres, Adebayor
24. 2006
25. 1979

ROUND 13 - THE REFEREE, RED CARDS AND RULES

1. 4
2. Pierluigi Collina
3. Three
4. Swiss
5. 1998
6. £375
7. 4
8. Claudio Caniggia
9. 1970
10. Paolo Di Canio
11. Stamp (1998), Head-Butt (2006)
12. 11 metres
13. Danish
14. Mark Clattenburg
15. 2010
16. Jens Lehman
17. 13
18. 1994, 2002
19. Stadio Olimpico, Rome
20. You could no longer be offside in your own half
21. Pep Guardiola
22. Brazil, Argentina, Uruguay
23. Rigobert Song
24. 7m x 2m
25. 2018

ROUND 14 - RECORDS

1. 2015
2. 34
3. 1999
4. Seven
5. Copa Del Rey, La Liga, UEFA Super Cup, Champions League, Spanish Super Cup, FIFA Club World Cup
6. Preston North End, Arsenal
7. Cafu
8. Wimbledon, Everton
9. 58 Metres
10. Lothar Matthaus
11. Luka Modric
12. 161
13. The Netherlands
14. Mark Schwarzer
15. 11
16. Tottenham Hotspur, Arsenal
17. 13
18. Arsenal
19. Jari Litmanen
20. Ian Wright
21. Lincoln City
22. Tammy Abraham
23. True
24. 91
25. Arsenal, Liverpool

ROUND 15 - SERIE A

1. Gianluigi Buffon, Paolo Maldini, Francesco Totti, Javier Zanetti
2. Roma
3. Michel Platini
4. 18
5. 2006-07
6. AC Milan, Juventus
7. Zlatan Ibrahimovic
8. Clarence Seedorf
9. Hernan Crespo
10. Sampdoria, Juventus
11. 11,000
12. 2011-12, 2012-13, 2013-14
13. Score 30+ goals in a Serie A season
14. Tottenham Hotspur to Lazio to Glasgow Rangers
15. Sven-Goran Eriksson
16. 16 years 242 days
17. 7 seasons, 1999 - 2006
18. Fabio Capello
19. £19.5 million
20. Lazio
21. Bonucci, Mandzukic, Higuain
22. 7
23. Kaka
24. Inter Milan, AC Milan, Atalanta, Juventus
25. Jose Mourinho

ROUND 16 - OTHER EUROPEAN COMPETITIONS

1. Arsenal (2), Middlesbrough, Fulham, Liverpool, Manchester United
2. Lazio
3. 2009-10
4. AC Milan, Sampdoria
5. Spain
6. 1960-61
7. 8
8. Chris Smalling, Marcus Rashford
9. Russia
10. Sevilla
11. Alaves
12. 2
13. Marseille
14. 7
15. €8.6 million
16. Celtic, Dundee United Rangers
17. Ronaldo
18. Dublin
19. Gus Poyet
20. Sevilla, Villareal
21. 1996-97
22. Manchester United, Arsenal, Chelsea
23. 1984
24. Monaco
25. 11-10

ROUND 17 - STADIUMS

1. Brentford Community Stadium
2. 40,000
3. Nou Camp, Wembley, Signal Iduna Park
4. Villa Park, Old Trafford, Hillsborough
5. Johan Cruyff Arena
6. Borussia Dortmund
7. Smoking
8. 1985
9. 10
10. Stade du Pays de Charleroi
11. 2005/2006
12. Estadio Azteca, Maracana
13. Tottenham Hotspur
14. Dundee, Dundee United
15. Soviet Union, Spain
16. False
17. Sunderland
18. 1990
19. Hamburg
20. 15
21. Millennium Stadium
22. Boundary Park (Oldham Athletic)
23. Vienna
24. Vale Park (Port Vale)
25. Jessica Ennis

ROUND 18 - PENALTIES

1. 1891
2. Alan Shearer (56)
3. Ivan Perisic
4. 21
5. 1982
6. When the first penalty is followed by the opposition taking two penalty kicks. This takes away any assumed advantage from going first throughout the shoot-out.
7. Dave Beasant
8. Roberto Baggio
9. Paul Ince
10. Blows the whistle and points to the penalty spot
11. Francesco Totti
12. Patrick Viera
13. 1976
14. His gloves
15. 1990
16. Marco Van Basten
17. Spain
18. USA (5)
19. 29
20. Paul Ince, David Batty
21. Bruce Grobbelaar
22. Obafemi Martins, Bobby Zamora
23. Germany, Argentina
24. Handled the ball on the line
25. Jorginho, Belotti

ROUND 19 - TRANSFERS

1. 1995
2. Ruud Gullit (£6 million)
3. Luis Figo, Zinidine Zidane, Kaka, Cristiano Ronaldo, Gareth Bale
4. Romelu Lukaku
5. Jonathan Woodgate
6. Kai Havertz
7. Gonzalo Higuain
8. £80 million
9. Lazio
10. Peter Schmeichel
11. Barcelona
12. Oscar
13. Mikael Silvestre, Danny Welbeck, Henrikh Mkhitaryan
14. Carlos Tevez
15. Sao Paolo, Real Betis
16. Chelsea
17. False
18. Sami Khedira
19. Miguel Almiron
20. Euro '96
21. Bari, Juventus, Sampdoria
22. Michael Laudrup
23. Free Transfer
24. Glen Johnson
25. 2017

ROUND 20 - AFRICA CUP OF NATIONS

1. Egypt
2. 1957
3. Germany, France
4. 9-8
5. 39 years, 174 days
6. Samuel Eto'o
7. 12
8. Guinea
9. 1960s
10. 2002
11. Nwankwo Kanu
12. 2000
13. Mike Smith
14. Frederic Kanoute
15. Hungarian
16. South Africa
17. 11
18. 2008
19. Rigobert Song
20. France
21. Benni McCarthy
22. 44 years and 21 days
23. Egypt
24. 1992
25. Gabon, Equatorial Guinea

Printed in Great Britain
by Amazon